ANIMAL BATTLES

CAMEL SPIDER VS. BLACK FAT-TAILED SCORPION

BY NATHAN SOMMER

BELLWETHER MEDIA • MINNEAPOLIS, MN

Torque brims with excitement perfect for thrill-seekers of all kinds. Discover daring survival skills, explore uncharted worlds, and marvel at mighty engines and extreme sports. In *Torque* books, anything can happen. Are you ready?

This edition first published in 2025 by Bellwether Media, Inc.

Library of Congress Cataloging-in-Publication Data

LC record for Camel Spider vs. Black Fat-tailed Scorpion available at: https://lccn.loc.gov/2024036215

Editor: Suzane Nguyen Designer: Hunter Demmin

Printed in the United States of America, North Mankato, MN.

TABLE OF CONTENTS

THE COMPETITORS

In the desert, small **predators** are on the hunt. Speedy camel spiders hunt whatever they find! **Prey** often cannot escape their powerful jaws.

Camel spiders compete for food with black fat-tailed scorpions. These scorpions can sting and defeat much larger prey. Which **arachnid** would come out on top in a fight?

Camel spiders are large arachnids. They grow up to 6 inches (15 centimeters) long, including their legs. They have hairy, tan bodies. Two long **pedipalps** sit near their mouths.

Camel spiders are found in deserts or dry areas around the world. They mostly hunt at night. Camel spiders stay underground during the day.

A TRICKY NAME

Camel spiders are not actually spiders. They belong to a group called solifugids.

CAMEL SPIDER PROFILE

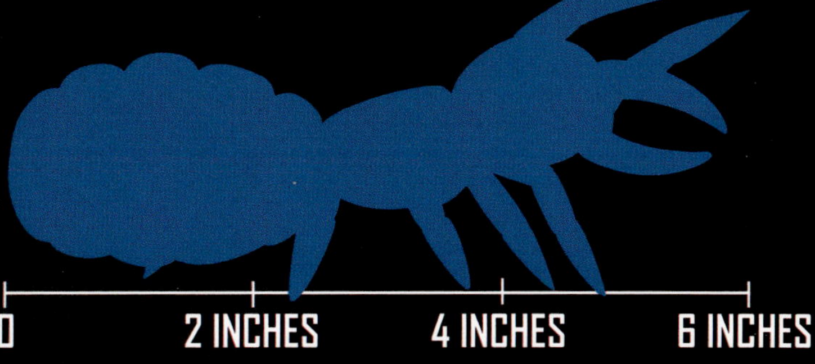

LENGTH
UP TO 6 INCHES
(15 CENTIMETERS)
INCLUDING LEGS

WEIGHT
UP TO 2 OUNCES
(57 GRAMS)

HABITATS

DESERTS

SHRUBLANDS

CAMEL SPIDER RANGE

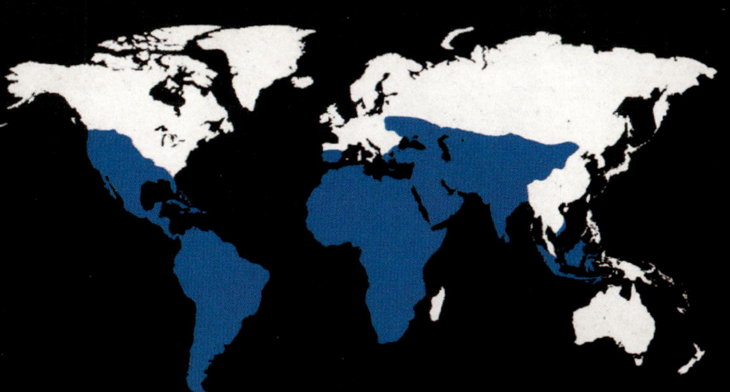

FAT-TAILED SCORPION PROFILE

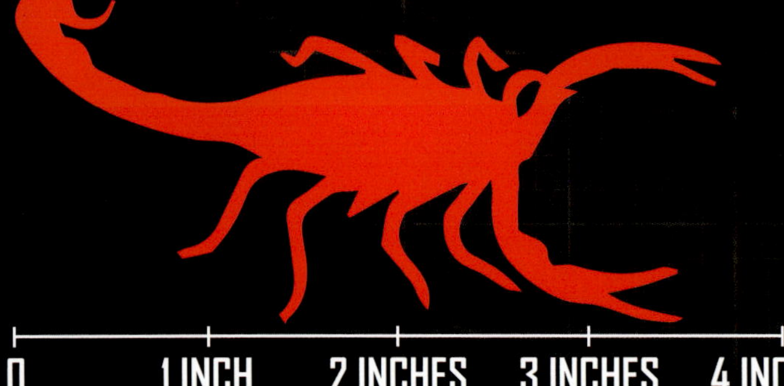

0 | 1 INCH | 2 INCHES | 3 INCHES | 4 INCHES

LENGTH
UP TO 3.5 INCHES
(9 CENTIMETERS)

WEIGHT (AVERAGE SCORPION)
UP TO 0.2 OUNCES
(6 GRAMS)

HABITATS

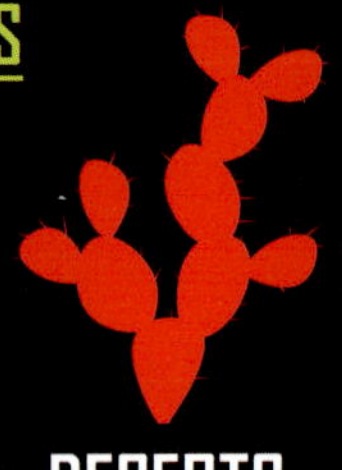

DESERTS

SHRUBLANDS

FAT-TAILED SCORPION RANGE

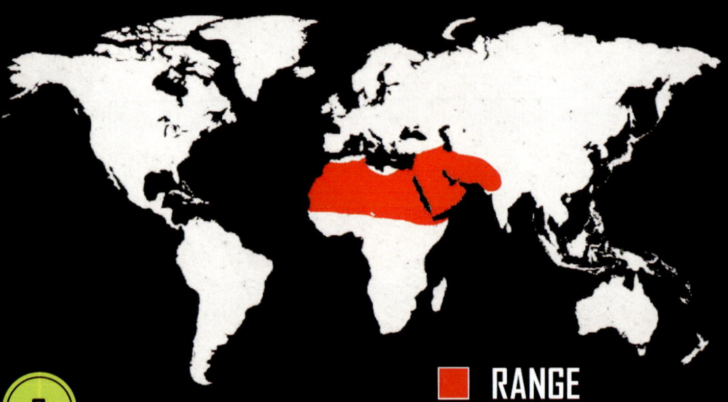

RANGE

Black fat-tailed scorpions are one of the most **venomous** scorpions in the world. They have sturdy black **exoskeletons** with large, thick tails. Their mouths have sharp **pincers**.

The scorpions are found in deserts of the Middle East and North and West Africa. They hide in cracks and under rocks during the day. This prevents them from drying out in the sun.

SECRET WEAPONS

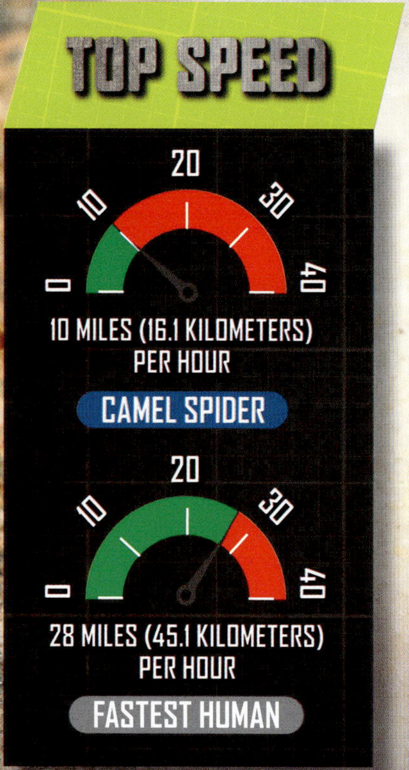

TOP SPEED

20
10
30
0
40

10 MILES (16.1 KILOMETERS) PER HOUR

CAMEL SPIDER

20
10
30
0
40

28 MILES (45.1 KILOMETERS) PER HOUR

FASTEST HUMAN

Camel spiders reach speeds of up to 10 miles (16.1 kilometers) per hour. The speedy hunters can run for hours at slower speeds without tiring. They quickly catch up to prey!

Black fat-tailed scorpions use their thick tails as weapons. The tails have sharp stingers on the end. They use them to strike enemies that come too close.

Camel spiders have long, powerful jaws. These can be one-third the size of their body. The sharp jaws are strong enough to cut small prey in half!

Black fat-tailed scorpions have a deadly venom in their stingers. They **inject** venom into prey to **paralyze** it. It also stops prey from breathing. This makes prey easier to eat.

SECRET WEAPONS

CAMEL SPIDER

SPEED

POWERFUL JAWS

DIGESTIVE FLUIDS

Camel spiders inject defeated prey with a **digestive fluid**. This turns the prey's insides into liquid. They can easily drink their meals this way.

BLACK FAT-TAILED SCORPION

SECRET WEAPONS

STINGER

VENOM

STRONG PINCERS

SMALL APPETITES

Black fat-tailed scorpions can survive for many months without eating.

Black fat-tailed scorpions use strong pincers to grab meals. The pincers easily crush prey. They also use them to hold prey in place while stinging it.

ATTACK MOVES

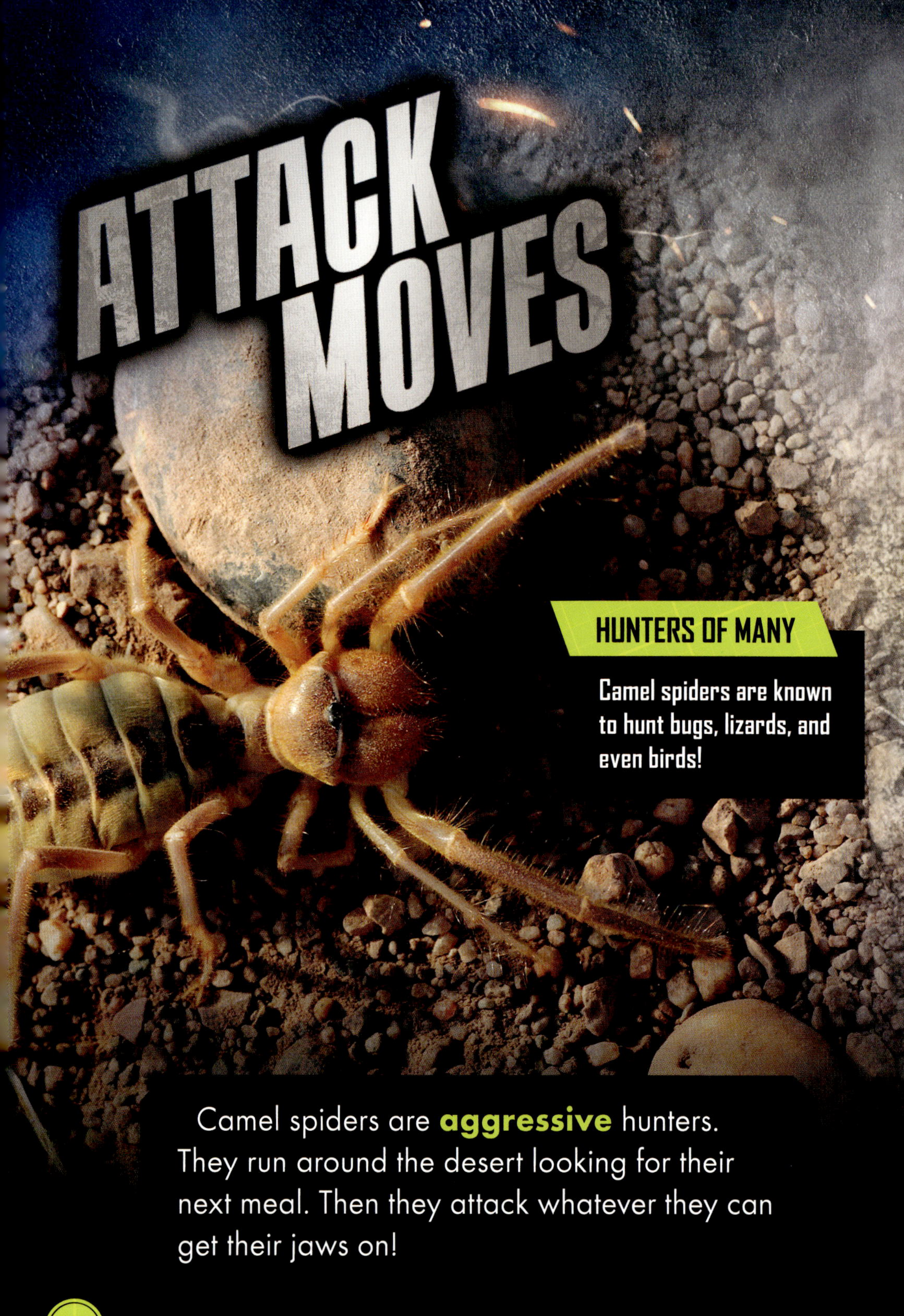

HUNTERS OF MANY

Camel spiders are known to hunt bugs, lizards, and even birds!

Camel spiders are **aggressive** hunters. They run around the desert looking for their next meal. Then they attack whatever they can get their jaws on!

Black fat-tailed scorpions hide in cracks with raised tails and open pincers. Then they catch and sting prey many times to defeat it.

Camel spiders use their long pedipalps to pull prey toward their mouths. Then they use their powerful jaws like a saw. This chops prey into smaller pieces!

LIQUIDS ONLY

Black fat-tailed scorpions are only able to eat food in liquid form.

Black fat-tailed scorpions crush small prey with their pincers. They use their stingers to paralyze larger prey. The venom helps turn the prey to liquid. The scorpion sucks up its meal!

READY, FIGHT!

A camel spider is looking for food. Suddenly, it is grabbed and stung by a hidden black fat-tailed scorpion! The camel spider fights back. It strikes the scorpion with its pedipalps.

The camel spider **lunges** at the scorpion with its powerful jaws. But it is defeated by the scorpion's venom before it can bite. The scorpion just scored a mighty feast!

GLOSSARY

aggressive—ready to fight

arachnid—an animal with two body segments and four pairs of legs

digestive fluid—a fluid that some arachnids use to turn the insides of prey into liquid

exoskeletons—hard outer coverings on some animals

inject—to force a fluid into something

lunges—moves forward quickly

paralyze—to make unable to move

pedipalps—small limbs used for grasping or feeling

pincers—curved claws with two sides used to grip things

predators—animals that hunt other animals for food

prey—animals that are hunted by other animals for food

venomous—able to produce venom; venom is a kind of poison made by some animals.

TO LEARN MORE

AT THE LIBRARY

Adamson, Thomas K. *Scorpion vs. Tarantula.* Minneapolis, Minn.: Bellwether Media, 2021.

Klatte, Kathleen A. *Scorpions at Night.* New York, N.Y.: PowerKids Press, 2021.

Mooney, Carla. *Insects and Arachnids.* Minneapolis, Minn.: Abdo Publishing, 2022.

ON THE WEB

FACTSURFER

Factsurfer.com gives you a safe, fun way to find more information.

1. Go to www.factsurfer.com
2. Enter "camel spider vs. black fat-tailed scorpion" into the search box and click 🔍.
3. Select your book cover to see a list of related content.

INDEX

The images in this book are reproduced through the courtesy of: kingma photos, front cover (camel spider); p. 5; Nature Picture Library/ Alamy, front cover (black fat-tailed scorpion), pp. 13, 15 (venom) (sharp stinger); Dmitry Fch, pp. 4, 16; Dr. MYM, pp. 6-7, 14 (digestive fluids); AnilD, pp. 8-9; ePhotocorp/ Getty, p. 10; blickwinkel/ Alamy, pp. 11, 15 (strong pinchers), 20-21; Dmitry Abezgauz, pp. 12, 14 (speed) (powerful jaws); Ondrej Michalek, p. 14; Carl Corbidge/ Alamy, p. 15; (c) Jacques Turner-Moss (CC BY-NC)/ iNaturalist UK, p. 17; SubAtomicScope, p. 18; ReptileMan27, p. 19; Jeff Kingma/ Getty, pp. 20-21.